Grasshopper had to have fun.

He had fun any way that he could.

1

When Grasshopper met Ant, he said,

"The sun is out.

It's a day for fun.

It's a day for me to jump and run!"

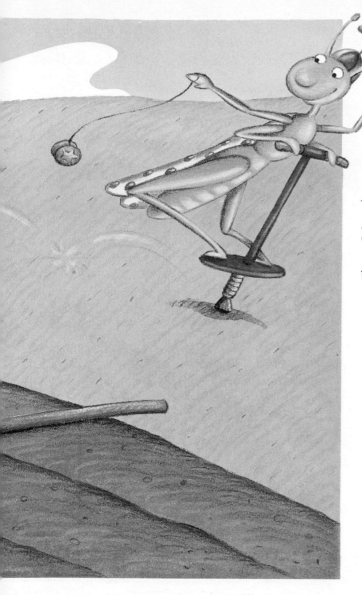

Ant had to plant.

She had to plant any way
that she could.

When Ant met Grasshopper, she said,

"The sun is out.

I have much to do.

I have to plant and that's fun, too!"

But one day Grasshopper
didn't jump and run.
He needed to eat more
than he needed to have fun.
"I'll go see Ant," he said.

Grasshopper could see Ant.

Now she was jumping and running.

And she had a lot to eat!

Grasshopper called to Ant,

"Let me in! I need to eat!"

Did Ant help Grasshopper?